Original title:
Tulip Temptations

Copyright © 2025 Creative Arts Management OÜ
All rights reserved.

Author: Eleanor Prescott
ISBN HARDBACK: 978-1-80566-754-4
ISBN PAPERBACK: 978-1-80566-824-4

Whispers of Spring

Beneath the sun, they giggle loud,
Twisting heads, they stand so proud.
Waving stalks, like dancers sway,
Whispering secrets, come what may.

Their petals bright, a playful tease,
Bouncing gently in the breeze.
Garden gnomes, they shake and cheer,
Promising laughs as spring draws near.

Allure in Color

Paint my garden with every hue,
Pink and yellow, oh what a view!
Dancing colors, what a sight,
Inviting bees to join the flight.

One cheeky bloom calls out to me,
"How about lunch, or maybe tea?"
But as I pause, it starts to sway,
It's "dinner time" for bugs today!

Garden of Yearnings

In the plot where dreams collide,
Petals giggle and never hide.
They plot a scheme, they brew some fun,
With each new bloom, their stakes are spun.

A dandelion makes a bet,
"I'll outshine you, just you bet!"
But all the hues just laugh and say,
"Together, we'll steal the show today!"

Radiant Hues

Colors burst like laughter's song,
In this garden, you can't go wrong.
Each petal tells a joke or two,
Where giggles flutter, skies are blue.

Hues parade, a lively crew,
Swapping tales, both old and new.
As bees join in the playful game,
They buzz and dance, it's all the same!

Blooming Allure Under the Sky

In a garden of colors, bright and bold,
The flowers conspire, secrets unfold.
They wiggle and giggle, a curious bunch,
Enticing the bees with a sweet little crunch.

With petals like skirts, they dance in the breeze,
Mocking the sun, saying, "Look at us, please!"
But watch where you step, it's quite a parade,
A stumble might leave you in flower brigade!

The Colorful Embrace of the Season

Those blooms with the blush and a flair for the fun,
  Inviting the daisies, they dance 'til they're done.
  They shimmy and sway in their vibrant delight,
  Making the tulips jealous of their party at night.

With a wink and a nod, they boast their bright hues,
"Can you match our style? Come on, give us your views!"

But blooms in a brawl? Now that's quite the show,
  It's a colorful tussle, with petals to throw!

Chasing the Sun-kissed Petals

As dawn starts to break, what a sight to behold,
The flowers awake, daring and bold.
They stretch out their arms, in cheeky array,
Chasing the sun, come join in the play!

With shades of pink laughter, and yellow delight,
They giggle at shadows that flee from the light.
But don't wear your flip-flops, you might lose your toes,
As petals fling laughter, oh how it just goes!

Scented Temptations at Daybreak

The morning is fresh with a floral surprise,
Petals whisper secrets, oh how they entice!
They tease the sweet air with a perfume so fine,
Amidst morning chuckles and spontaneous shine.

But the bees come a-buzzing, their dance is a blast,
"Did you see that one? Now that's quite the cast!"
It's a fragrance fiesta, a riotous scene,
Who knew that flowers could be such a queen?

Nectar of the Soul

In a garden, bees hold court,
Sipping nectar, quite the sport.
Flowers giggle, in their bloom,
Swirling colors, chasing gloom.

A butterfly slips, oh what a sight,
Dancing chaos, pure delight.
Leaves start laughing, roots can tease,
Whistling winds, such jolly breeze.

Shade of Enchantment

Under petals, secrets swirl,
Bumblebees in dizzy twirl.
Wind whispers tales of flower quirks,
While squirrels plot some silly works.

In the shade, a gnome does nap,
With a hat that's quite a gap.
A squirrel mockingly jumps and plays,
In a dance that never strays.

Vibrant Wishes

The colors clash with happy screams,
As daisies tease their fancy dreams.
Morning dew rolls down with glee,
While tulips boast of being free.

Sunshine giggles, clouds do pout,
Rabbits hop about, no doubt.
Wishes float on petals bright,
Bumbling bugs take flight with fright.

Blooming Charms

In a patch of vibrant blooms,
Worms hold parties, make their tunes.
Fluffy bunnies hop with grace,
Playing hide and seek with face.

Petals wink, and colors shout,
Frogs in chorus, croaking out.
A ticklish breeze makes flowers sway,
In this garden, joy will play.

Elegance of Nature

In gardens where colors sway,
Petals dance in bright array.
Bees with their humor, oh so bold,
Steal the sun's warmth, it seems quite cold.

A flower sneezes, pollen flies,
With laughter echoing through the skies.
Plants gossip with a rustling breeze,
While ants march by in tailored E's.

Blooming Secrets

Whispers of secrets in the air,
Dandelions tease without a care.
They giggle as you try to blow,
And leave you with a soft "hello!"

The roses plan a wild parade,
Where silly jokes are carefully laid.
Violets cringe from sunlight's glance,
As orchids slip into a dance.

Garden of Ecstasy

In the garden of laughter and cheer,
Where flowers bloom without a fear.
Petal jokes and whimsical sights,
What a delight on sunlit nights!

Sunflowers grin with golden might,
Chasing sunbeams with sheer delight.
A daisy dreams of being a star,
While teasing others for being bizarre.

Soft Allure

In beds of color, oh what a sight,
Petals blush, feeling quite light.
The tulips giggle, wearing their caps,
As rabbits hop with silly little flaps.

Whimsical winds sing softly sweet,
Inviting all to dance on their feet.
With laughter as bright as the blooms above,
Join the fun in the garden of love.

Garden of Seduction

In the garden where blooms sway,
Petals flirt in a silly ballet.
Bees buzz with a cheeky glee,
Winking at flowers, just like me.

Each bloom dons a bright, bold hue,
Laughing loudly in morning dew.
They whisper secrets, oh so sweet,
As butterflies waltz on tiny feet.

Roses roll their eyes in jest,
While daisies claim they are the best.
Sunflowers grin, towering high,
With stalks so tall, they touch the sky.

In this riot of colors amiss,
Join the flower party, can't resist!
With petals prancing, what a sight,
Laughter blooms from morning till night.

Petal Poetics

Oh! The petals dance in a chat,
A rose declares, 'I'm not that fat!'
Daffodils giggle, 'You're so vain!'
While violets chuckle, 'It's all in the grain!'

Underneath the sun's warm gaze,
Flowers wear their brightest phase.
Each one boasts of its grand style,
Turning heads with every smile.

Pansies wear hats that you'd adore,
While snapdragons snap just to score.
Laughter and perfume fill the air,
As petals sway without a care.

In the bloom of life, we find delight,
With a pop and a wink, we take flight.
Join the fun, in this petal prose,
Where laughter's the scent that always grows.

Serene Blooms

In the tranquil patch of green,
Blooms gossip, if you know what I mean.
Lavenders whisper with gentle grace,
While tulips giggle, 'We own this place!'

The daisies dance with the breeze in tow,
Making the sun go "Wow!" and the clouds go "Whoa!"
A sunflower checks its golden flair,
Says, 'Are you looking? Take a stare!'

With shades of yellow, pink, and blue,
Each flower competes for the best view.
It's a serene yet silly affair,
As petals ponder who's more rare.

Laughter echoes in this vibrant show,
As flowers flaunt with a cheeky glow.
Join the fun, take a wild leap,
In this garden where giggles never sleep!

The Call of the Bloom

Listen close; can you hear the calls?
As petals plot in the garden walls.
'Look at me!' the orchids boast,
While tulips blush, sipping tea like a host.

With every breeze, their antics grow,
Dancing like stars in a flower show.
A carnation cracks a wise remark,
While marigolds light up the park.

From morning dew to sunset gold,
These charming blooms are never old.
Like cheeky sprites with colors bold,
They weave sweet stories yet untold.

So heed the whispers in the sun,
Where flowers frolic, joy is spun.
Join the laughter, don't be shy,
In this blooming world, come laugh and fly!

Heartstrings of Flora

In gardens where the flowers play,
The bees all buzz in bright array.
They dance and twirl with zestful cheer,
While potted plants just drink their beer.

The daisies chuckle, oh so spry,
As dandelions float up high.
The roses roll their eyes in jest,
Claiming they're the fairest, yes, the best!

Sunflowers with their lofty hats,
Play peekaboo with chubby bats.
Each bloom has jokes tucked in their leaves,
And in the breeze, the laughter weaves.

So come, my friend, and have a look,
At flora's tales, they're quite the book.
In every petal, humor's sewn,
In this flowered world, we're never alone.

Lure of the Meadow

In the meadow, grass stands tall,
With ants hosting a grand gala ball.
The clovers giggle, hiding well,
From ladybugs with tales to tell.

The butterflies don't seem to care,
While enjoying gourmet air.
They flit and flutter, wearing grins,
And challenge bees for the best spins.

A lawn chair lies beneath the sun,
Where rabbits hop and ducks just run.
They share their secrets with a sigh,
While daisies wink with a sly eye.

In every corner, a story brews,
Of mischief and fun in vibrant hues.
So join the frolic, don't delay,
In meadows where the laughter stays.

Sway of the Garden

In the garden, flowers sway,
With sass that steals the whole display.
The orchids prance, the violets groan,
With petals flaring, proudly shown.

Throw in some weeds, a rambunctious crew,
They sing ballads of mischief too.
Counting the bugs that waddle and trot,
As if the garden's a grand hotspot!

The tulips blush, all painted bright,
Sharing secrets in the moonlight.
They crack jokes, oh what a tease,
While nightshade plants just shake their leaves.

In every swing and every twist,
Lies a fun-filled, fragrant twist.
Come take a stroll, let worries part,
Amidst the blooms, you'll find your heart.

Vivid Dreams in Bloom

In the dreamland where flowers sleep,
Petals whisper, secrets they keep.
Hibiscus dances with a flair,
While violets pop without a care.

The lilies wear crowns made of dew,
Swaying gently, just for you.
In this world, humor's the theme,
Where daisies plot their next great scheme.

Pansies snicker, plotting and prank,
And gardeners scratch their heads, then sank!
With each blossom, hilarity blooms,
As garden gnomes dodge plastic brooms.

So wander through this vibrant scene,
Where flowers flirt and laugh, so keen.
In every bloom, a jest awaits,
Join the fun and see their fates!

Celestial Garden

In a garden of dreams, where colors collide,
The flowers all giggle, and bees take a ride.
Zooming past petals, they swish and they sway,
While daisies do tap dance, they steal the day!

Oh, the roses are blushing, it's hard to believe,
They whisper sweet secrets, on this fine eve.
The sun winks at shadows, as clouds roll on by,
Bumblebees chuckle, as they zip through the sky.

Blossoms of Intrigue

Petals hold secrets, they giggle and tease,
In a game of hide and seek, if you please.
The daisies play poker, with pansies for chips,
While sunflowers gloat with their tower of tips.

Yet, in the moonlight, the daffodils prance,
Inviting the fireflies to join in the dance.
The garden's alive, with laughter and cheer,
And even the weeds are just sippin' their beer!

Charmed by Petals

Oh, the blossoms are cheeky, with plans so absurd,
They discuss all the gossip, like any good herd.
With shimmy and shake, vine rags on the floor,
They're throwing a party — who could want more?

Tulip in a hat, looking sharp as a tack,
Sipping on nectar, no need to hold back.
The violets compete for the crown of the night,
As the stars twinkle down, with sheer delight.

Captivating Colors

In a garden where colors clash,
Dancing petals make quite a splash.
Yellow sneezes, red will twirl,
Pink giggles in a floral whirl.

Bees in hats buzz on by,
Chasing blooms, oh my, oh my!
A butterfly trips on green's hue,
Exclaims, 'Why's it all so askew?'

Sunshine winks with a gleeful grin,
While flowers play, it's pure win.
Lavender whispers, 'Join the fun!',
As bees hum tunes under the sun.

Colors clash, a vibrant fight,
Blossoms giggle through the night.
Pollen floats like confetti in air,
Who knew gardens could be so rare?

Each flower sprinkles joy like confetti,
They sway and dip as if unsteady.
In this riot of shades, they conspire,
To spread laughter, the true desire!

Harmony in the Blossom

In a garden, chaos reigns supreme,
Flowers chatter, a comical dream.
Roses boast of their fancy clothes,
While daisies dance on their tiny toes.

Lilies roll their eyes in green shame,
'You call that beauty? What a lame game!'
But violets chuckle, 'Breakout the bling!'
For the fun lies where laughter can sing.

Poppies argue who has the best scent,
Daffodils laugh, 'We're heaven-sent!'
Butterflies join, their wings all a-flutter,
In this floral brawl, the joy's the utter.

Gardens thrive in glorious jest,
With colorful friends, it's truly the best.
In petals, hums, and silly pranks,
Laughter blooms in rows and ranks!

So come join their zany parade,
Where colors and giggles are lovingly laid.
Each bloom knows, with its vibrant power,
Joy is the heart of every flower.

Fragrant Serenade

A flower sings a silly song,
With scents that swirl and dance along.
Jasmine twirls with a fragrant glee,
Whispering secrets to the buzzing bee.

Petunias chuckle, 'Can you compete?'
With blooms so sweet, they take the seat.
Dandelions join with feathery puffs,
Saying, 'Our fluff is never enough!'

A bouquet of giggles fills the air,
While tulips sniff and fuss with flair.
But each knows, in their fragrant tune,
Laughter rises with the setting moon.

As sunlight fades, the flowers tease,
'We're the charms of nature's ease!'
With scents and smiles, they share the beat,
In this frenzy, isn't life sweet?

So next time you stroll through buds galore,
Listen closely, hear them implore:
Join their chorus of merry delight,
Where fragrance dances through the night!

Embrace of the Earth

With roots that tickle, buds that cheer,
The earth laughs, 'We're glad you're here!'
While marigolds tell tales of cheer,
Every bloom winks, 'No need for fear.'

Mud pies squish as flowers play,
'Let's cover the world in flower bouquet!'
A daisy shouts, 'May I take the lead?'
With petals all plump, their joy is freed.

From crooks of the earth to the sky so blue,
Each bloom shares laughs in vibrant hue.
Pansies giggle, 'Life's a pun!',
In the embrace of earth, we can have fun.

As rain joins in, a light-hearted jig,
The garden starts its grand, wet gig.
Fingers of grass reach high above,
In this embrace, there's laughter and love.

So join the dance, feel the soil's sway,
Where blooms and giggles embrace every day.
The earth's a stage for a joyful spree,
Together, let's bloom wild and free!

Swaying in Color

In a field of hot pink and bright sunny hue,
Flower dancers sway, oh what a view!
With petals that giggle and leaves that tease,
They wiggle and jive on a warm spring breeze.

One pranced too close to a passing bee,
"Buzz off!" she chirped, quite confidently.
The bee just buzzed with a cheeky grin,
As the flowers laughed, letting the fun begin.

Each bloom has a secret, a joke up its sleeve,
A tale of blossoms that we can't believe.
They whisper in colors, sharing a jest,
A parade of laughter, they're simply the best!

Come join the fun, don't be shy or shy,
In this silly flower game, we laugh and fly.
With every petal, a punchline will shower,
Swaying in color, laughing with power.

Echoes of the Meadow

In meadows so bright, where flowers confide,
The daisies tell tales, but the violets lied.
"I'm the best in the field!" boasted one bold bloom,
While the sunflowers chuckled, filling the room.

Their laughter, a chorus, so merry and spry,
As buttercups joined in, with a wink and a sigh.
"Who had the audacity to wear that big hat?"
The poppies chimed in, with a cackle and spat.

A ladybug stomped in, saying, "What's the fuss?"
While petals spun tales, causing quite the ruckus.
"I'll win the dance-off, just watch me swirl!"
As the flowers swayed, they twirled and twirled.

In echoes of laughter, this meadow's alive,
With blooms full of mischief, they dance and they jive.
So come for a giggle, stay for the cheer,
In this riot of colors, the joy's crystal clear!

The Colors of Affection

Petals in pink, they giggle and sigh,
While daisies compete in who's taller and spry.
"I'm the heart of the garden!" called one with glee,
"You're just a sidekick, if you ask me!"

The roses rolled laughter, a raucous delight,
"They may be all sweet, but we own the night!"
Each bloom claimed a crown, like royalty grand,
In this flower kingdom, no one's bland!

A tulip with bravado shouted, "I'm best!"
While petunias whispered, not giving a rest.
"Our fragrance is magic, it's charm we impart!"
With vibrant debates, they steal every heart!

So stroll through this garden, enjoy the charade,
Where colors collide in a joyous parade.
With laughter and love, we bloom and we play,
In this riot of romance, come brighten your day!

Glow of the Blossoms

The sun's shining bright on a dance floor of green,
Where blossoms are boogieing, oh what a scene!
Leave your worries behind, wear a smile like a crown,
As petals groove gently, never a frown!

One buttercup giggled, "Let's paint the sky!"
A burst of bright colors, oh my, oh my!
The violets chimed in, "With sparkles and cheer,
We'll douse the whole meadow, have nothing to fear!"

They twirled and they spun, in a colorful fray,
With blossoms that glimmered in the warm light of day.
A dance-off erupted; the bees took their stance,
As flowers and insects all joined in the dance!

So come to this party, the blooms spread the word,
With laughter and joy, it's happy birdword.
In the glow of the blossoms, we all find delight,
As colors unite in a fun, playful sight!

Garden of Yearning Hearts

In a plot of vibrant cheer,
The flowers nod, 'Come over here!'
They whisper sweet, enticing coos,
But watch your step, or you'll lose shoes!

With petals soft, they laugh and tease,
A dance of colors in the breeze.
But beware, the bees are keen,
They buzz about like they're on caffeine!

Sniffing scents that sweep the ground,
I tripped and fell without a sound.
The daisies giggled, just my luck,
In this garden, I'm truly stuck!

Though love may bloom in shades so bright,
These crafty blooms keep me in fright.
For in this patch, I've found my part,
A comedic play of yearning hearts!

The Seduction of Springtime Hues

Spring flaunts its colors, bold and brash,
With reds and yellows making a splash.
A flower parade, a sight so grand,
But watch your steps! Don't let them stand!

The violets wink with cheeky glee,
While lilies sing, 'Come dance with me!'
But while you twirl in floral bliss,
Watch out for pollen; you might just hiss!

The sunbeams laugh, it's quite the show,
While blooms boast of their lovely glow.
Yet amidst the beauty, there's one small fault,
A sneeze erupts! Oh, what a jolt!

Colors clash in a wild array,
As bees perform their aerial ballet.
In this spectacle of joys and blues,
I'm just a puppet to springtime hues!

Enchanted Bloom in Morning Light

Morning breaks with petals wide,
In this garden, let's take a ride!
But watch for thorns, they're sly and quick,
They'll steal a poke, just for a kick!

A daffodil shakes its golden head,
'Come join the fun, forget your bed!'
But when it dances, I rue the day,
I caught a bee and went astray!

The roses tease with fragrant ploys,
As I tiptoe, making some noise.
The tulips laugh, with their bold attire,
They're rascals too! We're caught in their fire!

Yet in this chaos, joy does bloom,
Even under the bees' wild zoom.
In morning light where we laugh and fight,
Life's a dance in this wild delight!

Frills and Thrills of Floral Whimsy

In gardens full of frills and thrills,
Petals twirl like playful quills.
A floral whimsy, such a sight,
As laughter blooms from morning light.

The marigolds play peek-a-boo,
While sunflowers flirt; it's quite the zoo!
I tried to count, but lost my place,
With all these frills, it's quite the race!

'Come dance with us!' the daisies shout,
But I tripped on roots, and roundabout!
With bees a-buzzing, caterpillars too,
Life's a riot in every hue!

So here I stand, knotted in greens,
With floral laughter in the scenes.
In this crazy garden, feelings bloom,
A frilly festival, dispelling gloom!

Forbidden Gardens of Delight

In gardens hid from prying eyes,
Petals dance in sly disguise.
Bees buzz low, gossip swift,
Flora's flirt is quite the gift.

Squirrels sip on nectar sweet,
Whispering secrets beneath their feet.
Laughter spills from every bloom,
While rabbits plot mischief, no room!

With every breeze, a chuckle sounds,
Nature's jest in leafy bounds.
The tulips wink, the daisies tease,
A riot of joy amongst the leaves!

Secret rendezvous in the shade,
Undulating fun, plans are laid.
Come join the folly, don't delay,
In this garden of cheeky play!

The Art of Blossoming Hearts

In a world where blooms conspire,
Hearts grow bright like flames of fire.
Every smile, a petal's grace,
Love is wobbly, like a vase!

Blossoms fidget in the light,
Trying hard to catch our sight.
With every sway, they hope to find,
A partner in this love so blind!

Butterflies are matchmakers at best,
Twisting twirls in colorful fest.
"Hey there, friend!" the daisies shout,
While tulips tease and dance about!

Hearts can bloom in a silly way,
With giggles soft as springtime's play.
Art of love, in nature's tune,
Draws joy like stars beneath the moon!

Echoes of Flora's Desire

In the meadow, secrets sprout,
With every laugh, a budding doubt.
Petals blush as secrets share,
Flora's whispers fill the air.

Roses roll their eyes so bold,
While violets giggle, stories told.
Every heart has its own flair,
Budding dreams, if you dare!

Crickets chirp the sweetest tune,
As flowers bounce beneath the moon.
"Let's sway and laugh," the blooms decree,
In a garden of glee, wild and free!

Softly sighs the evening breeze,
Laughter mingles with rustling leaves.
Echoes of joy, a floral spree,
Desires dance in harmony!

A Symphony of Shades

A canvas bright, where colors play,
Shades of giggles greet the day.
Each bloom a note, each laugh a song,
In nature's choir, we all belong!

Yellow smiles and purple sighs,
In this concert, humor flies.
With petals primed for friendly jests,
Every flower thinks it's the best!

Oh, how they flirt in splendid hues,
Making friends with the morning dews.
Each color sways in joyful beats,
While nature claps in soft retreats.

So join the blossoms in their flight,
Where laughter blooms from dawn to night.
A symphony where joy parades,
In a garden where fun never fades!

Soft Murmurs of Floral Fancies

In sunlit gardens, petals wide,
A bee buzzes by, with no place to hide.
It tickles the flowers, a giggle it brings,
As blossoms join in with their springtime flings.

A daisy blushed red, quite out of its mind,
It quipped to the rose, 'You're one of a kind!'
The tulips all danced in a daft little row,
Swapping their colors in nature's odd show.

The lily declared, 'I've got jokes to tell!'
While violets whispered their wishes so well.
They formed a tight circle, laughing with glee,
Sharing their dreams in a flowery spree.

Each petal a comic, with stories to share,
As nature's own jesters, who'd lighten the air.
So come, take a stroll through this whimsical plot,
Where flowers can giggle, and never do rot.

Caress of Nature's Touch

A breeze whispered softly, 'Hey look at me!'
As blossoms all fluttered, so wild and so free.
The petals turned blush at a joke from the sun,
'Can flowers wear shades? Well, this could be fun!'

A daffodil sneezed, then it giggled with pride,
While others all chuckled, no petals to hide.
'I've got pollen to share, but it's all just a tease,
What goes with a flower? Just add a few bees!'

The roses conferred beneath summer's bright glow,
'Who wears the best blush? Oh, come on, let's show!'
With petals all fluffed up, they strutted about,
Declaring, 'We're fab! There's no room for doubt!'

And daisies swayed in a rhythm divine,
'We're not just for kids—each bloom is a sign!
So let laughter ring out from gardens with mirth,
For nature's own jesters brightening earth.'

Petals of Desire

In the garden of giggles, where blooms love to tease,
A sunflower winked, 'Just look at us, please!'
With petals like dancers in colorful flight,
They twirled round the weeds in pure delight.

The tulips conspired with playful intent,
'Our colors are vivid—who's ready to vent?'
A poke from the lilacs, and off they all pranced,
Beneath the trees' watch, they hopped and they danced.

One daisy declared, 'I'm the queen of this plot!'
While others burst out, 'You're not all that hot!'
With laughter exploding like seeds in the breeze,
The garden became a raucous tease.

So when you stroll through this patch of delight,
Remember the bloomers, with jokes taking flight.
For flowers have stories, and humor entwined,
In petals of passion, sheer joy you will find.

Bounty of Blooms

A poppy exclaimed, 'Check out my bright hue!'
While daisies just giggled and joined in the view.
They formed a collage of colors and cheer,
As nature's own jesters, we gather right here!

The violets all whispered, 'We're shy, don't you see?'
'But who needs a show? Let's just be carefree!'
With petals all flopping in comical fun,
They jiggled and jostled 'til day's almost done.

The orchids were prim, but a twinge of surprise,
Made them join in the laughter, they'd try to disguise.
Their petals unfurled in the silliest way,
Creating a scene that brightened the day.

So come to the garden where humor takes flight,
Where blooms tell their tales with such colors so bright.
In this bounty of blooms, laughter's the key,
There's always more room for a giggle or three!

Mesmerizing Blooms on the Breeze

A flower shop on every lane,
Where fragrance feels like a sweet refrain.
Daffodil envy, oh what a scene,
Willy-nilly dances, they're so keen.

Petals whisper secrets from the ground,
Bumblebees buzz in circles around.
Sunshine tickles blooms so hard,
They giggle and wriggle, keeping guard.

Vases filled with color, oh what a sight,
Dancing shadows, all day and night.
Snapdragons laugh at what they can tease,
Each unfolding moment's sure to please.

In the garden, chaos reigns supreme,
Flowers plotting the wildest dream.
A sunflower winks, don't you dare stare,
This vibrant party's beyond compare!

Enigmatic Gardens of the Heart

In this patch of green, emotions bloom,
Garden gnomes plot in the twilight gloom.
Roses argue over who's the best,
While violets giggle, feeling quite blessed.

A daisy shyly peeks at the sky,
Wondering how and why flowers fly.
Hot peppers boast about spicy flair,
But tulips just blush, too cool to care.

Laughter lingers with each fragrant breeze,
Butterflies dance, doing as they please.
Whimsical weeds join in on the fun,
Making mischief until the day is done.

In this odd garden, the heart takes root,
Each silly petal dons a quirky suit.
Secrets spill like petals on the ground,
In these magical blooms, hilarity's found!

Petal Puzzles and Dreamy Gazes

A puzzle of petals in every hue,
The bees play chess, just for a clue.
With every turn, blooms take a chance,
As sunlit rays lead them in dance.

Hyacinths clash, who wears it better?
While dandelions share a brief letter.
"Breathe deeply," says one, "it's quite the game!"
A prickly cactus shouts, "Give me fame!"

In this dreamy maze where colors collide,
Buds and blooms, a whimsical ride.
Laughter weaves through fragrant air,
As petals drift down without a care.

Caught in a breeze, oh what a tease,
Nature's humor is bound to please.
Dancing blooms, with smiles so bright,
In this silly garden, all feels right!

Flourish of Love in the Air

Here love blooms in unexpected spots,
Among the daisies and playful pots.
Petals flutter, sharing sweet dreams,
As nature crafts in whimsical themes.

Tiny blooms whisper secrets and laughter,
While sunlight kisses, creating a chapter.
Roses tease with their glamorous stance,
Dipping into bloom balls, fancy dance!

Colorful patches, a jumble of cheer,
Bright blossoms beckon, "Come over here!"
In the garden, romance takes flight,
As beetles cue up for a late-night bite.

With each gentle sway in the playful air,
Love's a flower; hold it with care.
Laughter and petals flirt hand-in-hand,
In this quirky, love-filled flowerland!

Veils of Petals

In a garden so bright and bold,
Petals dance with stories untold.
A bee tries to woo, a flower to melt,
But ends up stuck, a first kiss felt.

With colors aglow, they twirl and sway,
Each whispering secrets of a sunny day.
A ladybug blushes, thinks it's in a show,
While grasshoppers giggle, at this floral tableau.

Pollen party, everyone's invited,
A balloon of a bee, nearly lighted.
But in the end, it's all just a jest,
As petals laugh while insects take rest.

In the riot of blooms, the mischief unfurls,
With laughter and joy, as nature twirls.
So if you stop by for a little hop,
Be ready for giggles, you'll never want to stop.

The Fragrance of Longing

A daisy sighs, with a hint of a dream,
A crush on the rose, or so it would seem.
But the thorny stem, such a rough guy,
Turns sweet looks to frowns, oh my, oh my!

The violets shudder, in shimmery clothes,
As their scent curls up, and gently bestows.
A longing for sunshine, a flirt with the sky,
Yet they all just pretend, as the days drift by.

In the air, a hope, a sweet little game,
Who will pick first? No one knows her name.
It's chaos of blooms, in their fragrant ballet,
With feelings so bright, yet clouded in play.

So stop and take in this vivid scene,
With winks and blinks, the garden's so keen.
For in the realm of petals, so grand,
Love's scent swirls round, a whimsical band.

Joyful Blossoms

Buds pop like popcorn, what a fine sight!
Stems twist and giggle, in sheer delight.
The daisies chime in with a jolly song,
While the sun peeks down, as if to belong.

A tulip trips over, what a grand fall,
It laughs and it rolls, with no shame at all.
Butterflies flutter, bartering charms,
As blossoms wave hands and show all their arms.

Each blossom's a joker, with tricks up their sleeves,
Making merry with laughter that nobody leaves.
In this carnival garden, a petaled parade,
The blooms all conspire, in whimsy displayed.

So step into spring, with a bounce and a twirl,
Among joyful blossoms, let your laughter unfurl.
For petals unite in this frolicsome scene,
Where flowers are silly and life's a routine.

Caress of the Breeze

The wind tickles leaves, and dances on grass,
While petals confetti, as crisp breezes pass.
A dainty bouquet, in hats oh-so-bright,
Giggling together, in the soft twilight.

Butterflies tease with a flirty display,
As bouquets compete in a silly ballet.
With each brush of wind, there's a fumble and fall,
Laughing, they rally, oh, what a ball!

A garden parade, where antics abound,
Where petals shake hands with a comical sound.
Who can resist such a breezy delight?
With whispers and chuckles, they twinkle at night.

So here's to the blooms, in their whimsical show,
Caressed by the breeze, they laugh as they grow.
Join in the fun, with a skip and a breeze,
For life's much too short, we do what we please!

Whispering Colors

In a garden dressed in hues,
Petals giggle in the breeze.
They gossip about the bees,
Taking sips like they're at a wine cruise.

Daffodils roll their eyes,
At all the tulips' flair.
"Look at us," they seem to share,
"While those fancy blooms just stare."

A polka dot dress, a floral tie,
Every bud's a fashion show.
They sway and twirl, oh my oh my,
Just watch them steal the whole tableau!

So grab a seat and take a peek,
At floral antics on display.
Laughing colors, vibrant, sleek,
Nature's jesters in a play.

Blossoms of Delight

Daisies chuckle, and roses tease,
Blooms gather round for a chat.
"Did you see the new bee?"
"I heard he's quite the acrobat!"

They swap silly stories and bright dreams,
A pollen party hard to beat.
Hilarious antics, bursting seams,
With laughter ringing from each seat.

A sunflower's joke goes very wide,
"Why don't plants ever go on vacation?"
"Because they love their roots, can't hide!"
The garden chuckles, a celebration!

So come, join the floral fun,
In fields where joy takes flight.
In a riot of colors under the sun,
Nature's laughter feels so right!

Secrets in Each Bloom

Petals whisper, secrets unfold,
Each flower has a tale to tell.
From pranky marigolds to bold,
Capers springing from each bell.

Daffodils peek while tulips pout,
"What's that noise?" they all ask.
"Oh, it's just the wind, without a doubt!"
While crickets join the floral task.

They scheme of walks and crafty schemes,
Sprouting jokes in morning light.
Sun-kissed laughter in dreamy dreams,
Nature's revelry takes flight.

So when you stroll among this crew,
Listen close, and join the fun.
In nature's realm, there's much to view,
Where every bloom is number one!

Nature's Lure

In meadows bright, where colors spry,
Each petal plays a playful game.
"Watch out! Here comes that pesky fly!"
And off they flutter, no one's the same.

The violets think they are the best,
While daisies laugh, they're carefree fools.
Whispers swirl like a floral jest,
Rooting for their teams, their blooms as tools.

A spin of yellow, a dash of pink,
They twirl around in gentle grace.
Running races; who'd ever think?
Nature's circus in this lovely place.

So if you're feeling blue or shy,
Just seek the garden's lovely view.
With every flower reaching high,
You'll find a chuckle waiting, too!

Petals of Desire

In a garden so bright and fair,
A flower tried to fix its hair.
With petals fluffed, it struck a pose,
But ah! There came a bee, who knows!

It buzzed and danced, a funny sight,
The flower blushed; oh what a fright!
It whispered 'Stay, don't fly away,'
But bees don't listen to what flowers say!

Each gust of wind sent petals flying,
The flower sighed, almost crying.
'Oh, can't you see? I'm quite the catch!'
Yet still, it felt a little scratch!

The sun peeped in, a cheeky tease,
And tickled petals with a breeze.
'Be bold!' it said, 'Don't hold back!'
But petals danced, all out of whack!

Whispers of Spring's Embrace

In the meadow, blooms in a row,
A daisy whispered, 'Look at me glow!'
'You think you're pretty, but I'm the queen!'
But wind just laughed; it loved the scene.

A host of colors, each wore a grin,
'Is that yours, or mine?' asked the lil' pin.
'Let's share the spotlight, it's pure delight!'
Then petals swayed in funny flight.

They giggled and danced under the sun,
Each bloomed for fun, just for a run.
A bumblebee joined the party too,
'Make way for me! I love the view!'

With every gust, they swirled away,
Causing a ruckus, come what may!
But laughter echoed as they spun,
In spring's embrace, all just for fun!

The Allure of Blooming Dreams

Once a bud with dreams so bright,
Stretched and yawned in morning light.
'Look at me! I'm destined to shine!'
But all it got was a pesky vine.

The vine wrapped round, quite like a hug,
'Let's grow together, you little smug!'
'Oh no, not you! I want the fame!'
But the vine just laughed and said, 'Same!'

As colors bloomed, they played a game,
Competing for sun; oh, what a claim!
'Who looks the best? I bet it's me!'
'Hold your petals! Let's wait and see!'

A butterfly landed, made a thought,
'Who's the fairest? Quite a lot!'
'Oh dear! What if I'm just a bore?'
And that's when dreams began to soar!

Colors of Enchantment

In a palette where colors collide,
A rose winked at a dandy side.
'With my charm, I steal the show!'
But then tripped over a garden hoe.

A daffodil giggled; oh what a sight,
'Doing fine, have you lost your light?'
'Not at all! Just a dance of grace!'
Then mud splashed on its bloom, what a case!

With laughter loud, the garden awoke,
Even the weeds decided to joke.
'We may not bloom in fancy hues,
But we make the best of these gardening blues!'

In colors bright, they found their flair,
Each bloom a joke, a playful dare.
In nature's joke, all hearts align,
For every petal, it's fun divine!

Fragrance of Enchantment

In the garden so bright, a bloom took flight,
Wiggling its leaves, it danced through the night.
All the bees buzzed, a comical sight,
Chasing sweet nectar, oh, what a delight!

With petals so soft, it gave a sly grin,
Inviting the critters to come in and spin.
A flower's charm, drawing all with a grin,
While squirrels protested, 'It can't be a win!'

The colors so vivid, a riot of cheer,
Each shade tells a tale that we'd all love to hear.
Hungry rabbits ponder, 'Should we nibble here?'
While daisies roll their eyes, 'We know why you're near!'

But in the end, it's all such a joke,
That bloom laughs aloud, making shadows provoke.
In this fragrant theater, we're all just smoke,
In a garden so wild, where laughter awoke.

A Story in Petals

Once a petal didn't know it was bright,
But then a breeze whispered, 'You're quite the sight!'
It twirled on the stem, oh, what a delight,
Flaunting its colors with all of its might!

A ladybug chuckled, 'You're hard to ignore,
Acting so fancy, but what's at your core?'
The petal just giggled, 'I'm here to explore,
Life's just a giggle; I'll always want more!'

A tale in each layer, a drama unfolds,
Of roses and violets, the stories they told.
When wind came a-swooping, the laughs would unfold,
As petals got tangled, their secrets went bold!

So join in the fun, let laughter take flight,
In gardens of mischief, everything's light.
With stories in petals, oh what a sight,
Even the insects are giggling tonight!

Temptress of the Garden

She sways in the breeze, a sly little tease,
Her colors so bold, bringing insects to knees.
With whispers of fragrance, she plays with her ease,
Oh! Fluttering hearts, she'll aim to appease!

Bumblebees plot their sweet serenade,
While snails in tuxedos wish they were displayed.
'Round her they gather, all charmed and betrayed,
Their waltz grows frantic as laughter gets made.

The tulips cackle, 'Oh darling, you sly!
You've got all the bugs flying high in the sky!'
But she just giggles, 'Give it a try,
Garden's a stage, let your dreams say goodbye!'

So if you should wander the floral domain,
Beware of the temptress, all fun and insane.
With a wink and a nod, she'll dance in the rain,
In a garden of giggles, where we're all entertainment!

Dance of Color

A party of hues is what we can see,
Reds flirt with yellows, so jovially free.
Each petal a dancer, oh, what jubilee!
Swirling and twirling, pure glee in the spree!

The daisies are laughing, 'Look at that show!
Who knew colors could put on a glow?'
With winks and with nods, they put on the flow,
In shades of pure joy, it's quite lovely, you know!

The butterflies flutter with steps that delight,
While ladybugs jive in their charming attire.
Together they mingle, creating on sight,
A dance of confusion, oh, such a sight!

So join in the whirl, let your colors run free,
In a garden explosion, just dance with glee.
For in this grand ballet, it's clear to see,
Life's a vibrant dance, and you're one with the spree!

Essence of Delight

In a garden, blooms a sight,
Colors dance in morning light.
Bees are buzzing, all a-flutter,
Careful now, don't step in butter!

With petals bright, the bees make rounds,
A sneezing fit? Oh, hear those sounds!
A butterfly with legs that slip,
Takes a tumble—what a trip!

Sun hats on, we laugh and play,
Who knew blooms could lead astray?
With cheeks so rosy, smiles wide,
In this park, we laugh and glide!

So here's to blooms that make us grin,
Let the antics of nature begin!
In this playful floral chase,
We find laughter in this place.

Petal-Kissed Moments

Oh look! A flower's mid-air flight,
Chasing petals, what a sight!
Caught a whiff of pollen's tease,
Now I'm sneezing—oh, such ease!

A gardener trips, and oh my,
Dirt flies up, but spirits high!
With muddy shoes and grimy hands,
Who knew gardening's so grand?

The sun is shining, birds do sing,
Who knew plants could be such a fling?
In this field of bustling cheer,
Come on, friends, let's all draw near!

So twirl around the blooms so bright,
With petal-kissed laughter, pure delight.
We'll take a snapshot; what a scene,
In our flower-crowned hearts, we've been!

Palette of Spring

With colors splashed in yellow and pink,
This garden makes me stop and think.
The flowers giggle, the shrubs wear grins,
What a circus this spring begins!

A rogue wind steals a hat away,
Chasing petals, come what may.
And as I reach, I trip and flop,
Now I'm part of this floral hop!

Pansies wink, and daisies cheer,
'Join the fun, we're glad you're here!'
With every step, we laugh and play,
In this riotous floral display.

So let's paint our lives with colors bright,
In this canvas of laughter and light.
Nature's a joker with blooms so spry,
Join the palette, give it a try!

Romance in the Garden

Beneath the arch of creeping vines,
I'll serenade you with sweet lines.
Looks like a rose just spilled its tea,
Hold my hand, let's make it three!

A bumblebee hums a tune so fine,
With such charm, it must be divine!
A ladybug prances, dressed in red,
Making sure it's well-spread ahead.

We dance between the daffodils,
Who knew romance could bring such thrills?
With petals falling like confetti's grace,
This garden's turned into our place.

Let's toast to blossoms and laughter bright,
In this secret grove, love feels just right.
With every bloom and every quirk,
We find delight in nature's work!

Ecstasy of the Garden

In the garden, blooms stand tall,
With colors bright, they have a ball.
Petals dance in a breezy sway,
While bees buzz around for a play.

Worms in soil hold their grand parade,
To the rhythm of the flowers' charade.
Roses giggle, lilies snicker,
Every bloom is a happy trickster.

Sunlight tickles the leaves with glee,
Each blossom smiles, and so do we.
A spider spins tales of blissful jest,
In this wild garden, we are blessed.

Watch out for the winking daisies,
Enticing us with their whimsical hazies.
With laughter echoing in this scene,
The fun in flowers is evergreen!

Lush Exuberance

A patch of daisies plotted mischief,
With petals soft as a sweetened dish.
Lilacs whisper secrets all around,
As sunflowers grin, they wear the crown.

Butterflies search for the comfiest seat,
On zinnias that cannot be beat.
Pansies chuckle, violets tease,
While garden gnomes just try to please.

Weeds join in for a wild card game,
Roots intertwined, they're all the same.
Sharing riddles as the crickets chirp,
Nature's laughter makes our hearts burp.

Freckles of color in every view,
The garden's a party, it's not just a clue.
So come and laugh under the sun,
In this land of petals, let's have some fun!

The Garden's Seduction

A rose winked at a shy marigold,
Promising tales of warmth untold.
Lilies strut like they own the lane,
While dandelions puff clouds of gain.

The tulips laugh at the morning dew,
Playing tricks, as they stay so true.
Hostas hum a purring tune,
Underneath the chuckling moon.

Grasshoppers jig on a leafy stage,
With ants joining in without a cage.
Every petal dashes, every leaf runs free,
In this secret garden, it's all a spree.

So gather your giggles, it's time to frolic,
Where blooms create mischief, oh so symbolic.
With every color that catches the eye,
This wild garden makes laughter fly!

Colorful Whispers

Petals whisper in the softest tones,
As butterflies dance on their leafy thrones.
The marigolds chatter with much delight,
While bees plot their honey-filled flight.

Poppies pop and sing a cheeky tune,
Under the watchful stare of the moon.
Frolicking ferns joke with ease,
As the weathervane spins in the breeze.

Each blossom has tales of laughter and cheer,
Sharing secrets that only they hear.
A garden party filled with giggles and prance,
Inviting all critters to join in the dance.

So gather around for this bloom-filled jest,
Where joy is abundant and nature is best.
In colors so bright, with a wink and a grin,
The garden's story of fun can begin!

Secrets Beneath the Soil

In the garden, secrets hide,
Worms gossip while roots collide.
The flowers giggle, oh so sly,
"Let's plant a rumor, watch it fly!"

Bees buzzing with tales to share,
A romance blooms with fragrant air.
But what's that scent? A dirty sock?
The garden blushes, tick-tock, tick-tock!

Radiance in a Sea of Petals

In colors bright they turn and twirl,
Like actors in a floral whirl.
A daisy winks, a rose blushes,
While tulips argue—who's the fluffiest?

Butterflies dance in a dizzy spree,
"Is that a flower or just me?"
Petals toss their heads in pride,
While bees offer... a honeyed ride.

Sweet Nothings in Bloom

A dandelion spills some tea,
"I'm sweet as honey, can't you see?"
The petals lean in, ears aglow,
"Tell us more, we love your show!"

But wait, what's that? A carrot's blight?
"Oh dear! Hide, everyone—goodnight!"
The laughter fades, a hush, then cheer,
A blooming prank is always near!

Serenade of the Colorful Fields

In fields of color, joy takes flight,
A tulip's serenade, what a sight!
"Do you hear that?" a bloom will tease,
"It's not the wind; it's laughter's breeze!"

A peony strikes a pose so grand,
"I'm off to dance, will you join the band?"
But oh, the sun, a jokester bright,
"Careful, friends, I control the light!"

Frescoes of the Landscape

In fields so bright, they dance and play,
With colors bold, they steal the day.
Little heads bob, a comical sight,
Swaying to the wind, with all their might.

Their petals wide, like laughter loud,
Fashioned from sunshine, so picturesque crowd.
Giggling stems join in a silly race,
Who knew blooms could have such grace?

Bumblebees buzzing, a happy tune,
They waltz with buds beneath the moon.
One flower tips, like it's had too much,
Toppling over with a gentle touch.

So here we stand, with glee so grand,
In this garden party, we've all planned.
Nature's jesters in a riotous spree,
A sunny parade, just you and me.

A Symphony of Blooms

A patchwork quilt of petals bright,
Stitching the ground in laughing light.
Each one sings with a silly cheer,
A symphony of blooms, my dear!

They wiggle and jiggle, a vibrant show,
Who knew flowers had such a glow?
Caterpillars sigh, feeling quite small,
Caught in the antics of them all.

One cheeky bloom dons a hat of green,
Pretending to be the garden queen.
With a twirl and a giggle, she spins her tale,
As raindrops join in, a comedic hail.

While bees conduct in their funny way,
Drumming on petals, come what may.
With every buzz, a chuckle shared,
In this wild concert, we're all declared.

Vibrant Intrigues

A mystery hides in every bloom,
Is it a flower or a bouncing broom?
Each shade a plot twist in disguise,
In this quirky garden, surprises rise!

Ladybugs giggle on a petal's edge,
Sipping the nectar of their pledge.
Who needs a ball when there's pollen to chase?
These tiny actors find perfect place.

Petals whisper secrets, quite absurd,
Could they be telling tales of the bird?
With a rustle and shake, they plot and plan,
Filling the air with laughter's span.

In this realm, joy takes its course,
With bubbles of laughter, wild as a horse.
A fiesta of colors, and a tickling breeze,
This garden of humor—it surely does please.

Euphoria in Bloom

In a riot of colors, the laughter flows,
Bright blooms bounce like little shows.
Chasing the sun with petals so bold,
A festival of joy, pure and uncontrolled.

Dancing ants in wiggly lines,
Gathering friendships, sipping on wines.
Each squiggly worm wears a smile so wide,
A disco's play in nature's hide.

With rainclouds chuckling above our heads,
They sprinkle joy, as blooming spreads.
What fun is this, a playful deluge,
Of colors and laughter in a happy refuge?

Amongst the giggles of flowers sweet,
Life's silly march carries on with beat.
Every petal whispers, "Join the fun!"
In this garden's laughter, we all are one.

Enchanted Meadows

In a meadow full of blooms,
Bees are buzzing, making zooms.
A flower wears a silly hat,
While butterflies laugh, just like that!

Daisies peek with a wink so sly,
Silly petals waving goodbye.
A sunflower giggles, tall and bright,
Chasing shadows with pure delight.

Grasshoppers dance with leaps so grand,
While petals join in a wild band.
Nature's laughter fills the air,
In this meadow, joy is everywhere!

With every bloom, a giggle's found,
In enchanted meadows, fun abounds.
So take a step, embrace the cheer,
And let the flowers whisper, dear!

The Language of Flowers

In gardens lush, where flowers chat,
Roses blushing, having a spat.
Petunias gossip, oh what a thrill,
While tulips join in, against their will!

A daffodil shouts, 'I'm the best!'
While daisies giggle, 'We pass the test!'
Orchids sigh with a graceful pose,
'We speak only of love, or so it goes!'

Floral whispers turn into yells,
As marigolds share their secret spells.
Sunflowers nod, trying to lead,
But pansies just laugh, 'Oh, yes indeed!'

In this vibrant dance of floral jest,
Every bloom thinks it's better than the rest.
So tune your ears and hear them play,
The language of flowers brightens the day!

Senses in the Garden

In a garden bursting with delight,
Colors flaunt in pure sunlight.
Scented breezes tease the nose,
While petals blurt out silly prose!

Sensory overload, oh what a show,
Taste the pollen, just don't let it grow!
The colors tickle, oh what a thrill,
As flowers sway with exuberant will.

Listen closely, you'll hear them cheer,
As garden gnomes whisper, 'Come near!'
Textures galore, soft as a dream,
In this floral world, we all beam!

Senses merge in a wacky waltz,
Blossoms tease, never come to a halt.
Such delightful nonsense, can you see?
In the garden of laughter, we're all free!

Floral Temptations

Oh, the flowers flaunt their hues,
With petals soft, they share their views.
Rose just winked, a cheeky flirt,
While violets giggled in the dirt.

Every bloom has a funny tale,
From daisies prancing to lilies pale.
Marigolds argue who's the best,
While zinnias laugh at their little jest.

In this patch, no one can pout,
Every color wants to shout.
So join the party, come and sway,
In floral games, we laugh all day!

With every petal, humor grows,
As nature serves up her silly shows.
In this playful garden, come partake,
Where flowers tease, and laughter wakes!

Lured by Nature's Palette

In shades so bright, the flowers play,
Their colors tease from day to day.
I tiptoe close, I stop and stare,
Who knew blooms could have such flair?

The daisies giggle, the roses wink,
While naughty violets plot and think.
They whisper tales of scents divine,
"Come join our party, sip the brine!"

The tulips twirl in breezy glee,
"Behold our beauty, come drink with me!"
But as I reach for petals bold,
A bee buzzes in, I'm shooed, I'm told!

With laughter blooming, we all collide,
In nature's hues, we dash and slide.
I'm lured by blooms that dance and sway,
In this garden of giggles, I'll surely stay!

Velvet Vows in the Garden

Among the greens, oh what a sight,
Velvet petals in morning light.
They vow to charm with every sway,
But I just tripped – oh what a play!

With every breath, a fragrant tease,
The blooms erupt like kindly bees.
"I'm here, I'm here!" they sing and shout,
While I pretend to dance about.

A dandy lion takes a bow,
"Join us, human, we'll show you how!"
I spin and twirl, I nearly fall,
The garden chuckles, I hear them call!

In velvet vows beneath the sun,
All blooms unite for extra fun.
With petals soft and laughter bright,
The garden burst, a sheer delight!

Captivating Fragrance of Dawn

Morning waves a fragrant hand,
While flowers giggle, take a stand.
Their scent bewitches with a cheer,
"Come closer, friend, don't disappear!"

The lilies laugh, they sway and swoon,
Their perfume floats beneath the moon.
"I'm sweet," says one, "I'm oh so bold!"
But watch your step, or you'll be sold!

A hapless bumblebee drops in,
A pollen party now begins.
I join their winged, hilarious plot,
But zooming bees – oh, what a lot!

Dawn unfolds with nectar bright,
With every bloom, it feels just right.
I laugh and dance, what a delight,
In this garden, my heart takes flight!

Dances of Flowering Secrets

In petals soft, secrets abound,
Each bloom a whisper in sweet sound.
"Shhh, come closer, we won't bite!"
The daisies grin, the scene's just right.

A wiggly stem does a little jig,
While bees perform a buzzing gig.
"Oh don't mind us, we're just a tease,
Stay for the fun, we aim to please!"

With colors bold and laughter free,
They host a dance for all to see.
Petals flutter, I find my place,
In this wacky, flowery embrace.

The secrets shared in whispered hues,
With every step, I chase the clues.
In blooming antics, joy abounds,
I'll keep dancing with flowered sounds!

www.ingramcontent.com/pod-product-compliance
Lightning Source LLC
Chambersburg PA
CBHW051634160426
43209CB00004B/646